IN THE
GARDEN

Richard Powell and Steve Cox

Baby's First Book Club

I spy
with
my
little
eye

something beginning with

S

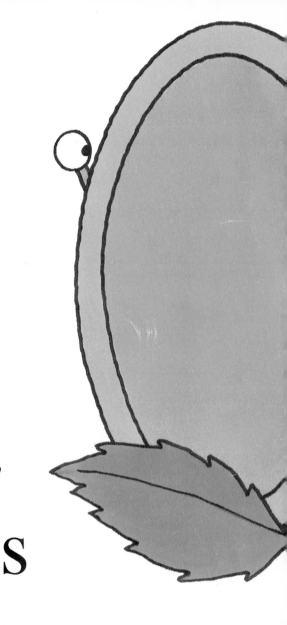

I spy
with
my
little
eye

something beginning with

r

abbit

I spy
with
my
little
eye

something beginning with

W

I spy
with
my
little
eye

something beginning with

b

orm

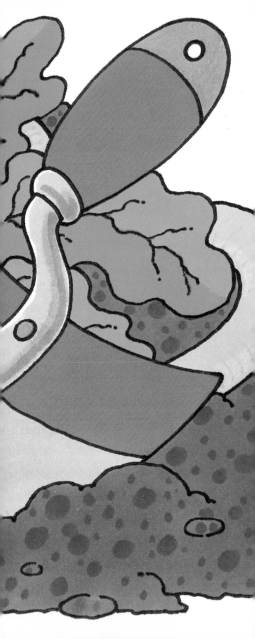

utterfly

I spy
with
my
little
eye

something beginning with

c

at

I spy
with
my
little
eye

something beginning with

W

heelbarrow

I spy
with
my
little
eye

something beginning with

b

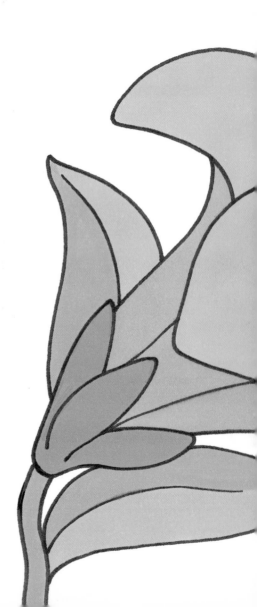

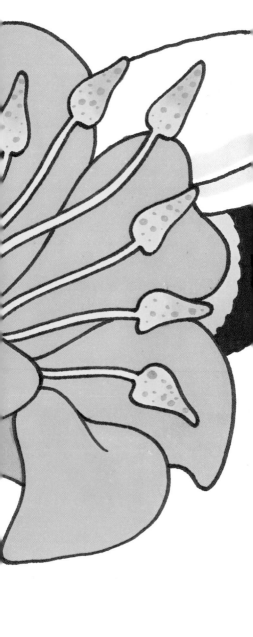

ee

I spy
with
my
little
eye

something beginning with

g

nail

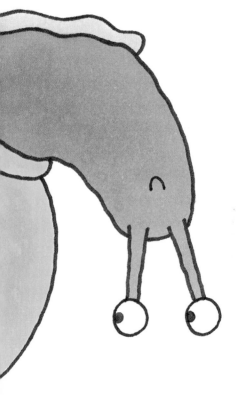

oldfish

I spy
with
my
little
eye

something beginning with

l

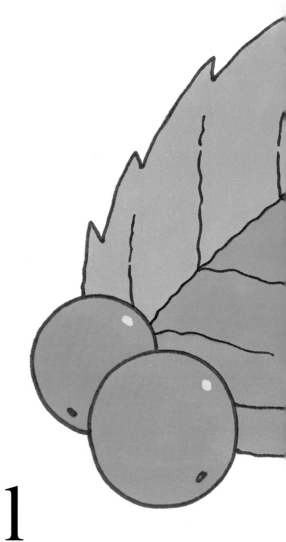

adybug

I spy
with
my
little
eye

something beginning with

c

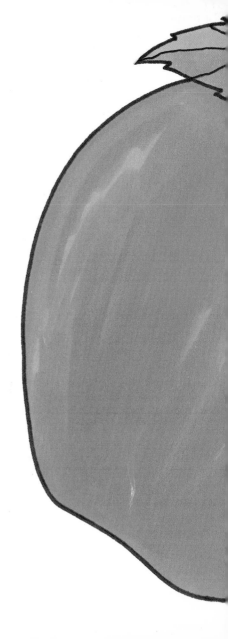

aterpillar

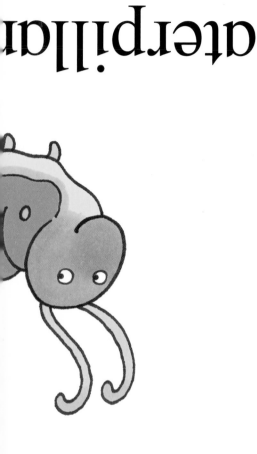

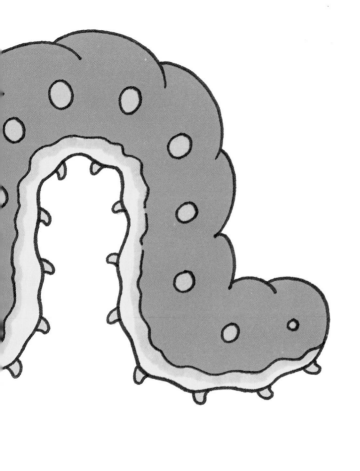

I spy
with
my
little
eye

something beginning with

d

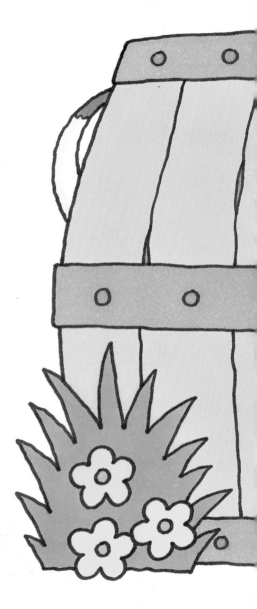